Microsoft Word for Beginners

A 7-Day Essential Guide to Mastering Word
Features, Commands, Shortcuts, Tips, and Tricks

Aaron J. Reiss

ISBN-13: 9798326920638

DEDICATION

To every one of my readers!

TABLE OF CONTENT

Introduction

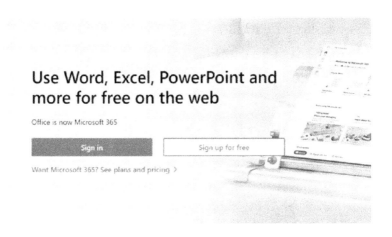

Embarking on the journey of mastering Microsoft Word opens doors to a world of possibilities in document creation and editing. Whether you're a student, professional, or someone seeking to enhance their digital literacy, Microsoft Word stands as a cornerstone tool for crafting polished and professional documents.

First and foremost, understanding the fundamental layout of Microsoft Word is key to navigating its myriad features seamlessly. The interface typically comprises a ribbon at the top, housing various tabs such as Home, Insert, Page Layout, References, Mailings, Review, and View. Each tab is packed with tools and functions tailored to different aspects of document creation and formatting.

One of the standout features of Microsoft Word is its versatility in handling different types of documents. Whether you're drafting a simple letter, creating a detailed report, designing a flyer, or formatting a resume, Word provides the tools and templates to meet your needs. This flexibility makes it a go-to software for a wide range of writing and design tasks.

Moreover, Microsoft Word's robust editing and formatting capabilities empower users to customize their documents with precision. From adjusting margins, fonts, and colors to inserting images, tables, and hyperlinks, the possibilities for creating visually appealing and professional-looking documents are virtually endless.

In today's digital age, compatibility and accessibility are paramount. Microsoft Word excels in this aspect by offering compatibility with various file formats, including ".docx," ".pdf," ".rtf," and more. This compatibility ensures that your documents can be easily shared, opened, and edited across different devices and platforms.

Furthermore, Microsoft Word is equipped with tools for enhancing document accuracy and professionalism. Spell check, grammar check, and formatting consistency tools help users maintain high standards of quality in their documents. These tools are particularly beneficial for ensuring error-free and polished content.

Accessibility features in Microsoft Word also deserve mention. The software provides tools for creating accessible documents, such as alt text for images, headings for document structure, and keyboard shortcuts for navigation. These accessibility features ensure that your documents are inclusive and accessible to all readers.

In summary, Microsoft Word is not just word processing software; it's a versatile tool that empowers users to create, edit, collaborate, and present documents with ease and professionalism. Whether you're writing a simple memo or crafting a complex report, Microsoft Word's robust features and intuitive interface make it an indispensable tool for anyone working with digital documents.

Chapter 1: Getting Started

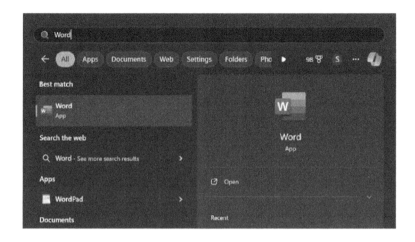

1.1 Getting Microsoft Word for Free

By following these suggestions, you might be able to cut your expenses by $100 per year.

Microsoft 365 represents the latest iteration of the Microsoft Office suite, incorporating familiar programs utilized in everyday life, whether it's for personal, educational, or professional purposes. Among these programs are PowerPoint, Outlook, and Word. Purchasing a Microsoft 365 subscription remains the preferred method for gaining access to these tools and additional functionalities.

As of January 11, 2023, Microsoft unveiled the launch of Microsoft 365 Basic, priced at $2 per month or $20 for an annual subscription. Nevertheless, there are certain situations where you can obtain Microsoft 365 for free.

Microsoft's collection of productivity software includes timeless favorites such as Outlook, PowerPoint, Excel, and Word, alongside newer applications like Microsoft SharePoint, OneDrive, and Teams.

The suite usually comes with a price tag ranging from $20 to $100 per year, granting subscription access across multiple devices and for family members. Additionally, Microsoft offers a standalone version of Microsoft Office for Mac and Windows users named Office Home and Student 2021, available for a one-time fee of $150 without the need for a subscription.

Here are the available versions of Office 365, Microsoft 365, and other sister applications that you can access at no cost.

1.1.1 Free Microsoft Office 365 Education for Teachers and Students

If you are a teacher or a student, you can get Microsoft Office 365 Education for free.

Microsoft Teams, OneNote, PowerPoint, Excel, Word, and other classroom tools are all included in Office365, which is available for free from Microsoft if you're a student, instructor, or staff member with an active academic email address.

Simply enter your school email address on Microsoft's Office 365 Education webpage. In most instances, you'll gain immediate access through an automatic verification process. However, if your school requires verification, it could take up to 30 days to validate your eligibility.

College students with a valid school email address can access Microsoft 365 Personal for a monthly fee of $3.

1.1.2 Free Microsoft Office for Everyone

If you're anyone else, you can obtain the Microsoft Office suite for free.

You can sign up for a 1-month Microsoft 365 free trial, but you'll need to provide your credit card details. If you do not cancel the subscription before the trial ends, you will be charged $100 for a 1-year subscription to Microsoft 365 Family, previously known as Office 365 Home.

If you don't require the entire Microsoft 365 suite, you can still use several of its apps for free online. These apps include Clipchamp, Designer, Skype, My Content, Calendar, Outlook, OneDrive, PowerPoint, Excel, and Word. Here's how to access them:

- Visit Microsoft365.com.
- Click on "Sign up for the free version of Office," located beneath the "Sign in" button.
- Sign in to your Microsoft account or register a new one for free. If you use Xbox Live, Skype, or Windows, you already have a Microsoft account.
- Choose the application you need, and store your projects on OneDrive in the cloud.

1.1.3 What is the Catch with the Free Version?

You might wonder, "Why pay for Microsoft 365 when I can access those applications for free?" Well, the free versions have limitations. They work only in your web browser and require an active internet connection. Plus, they offer a small number of features compared to the all-inclusive Microsoft 365 versions.

The free version still has some advantages, such as sharing work links and real-time collaboration, similar to Google Workspace tools. If you need basic app versions, the free option should suffice.

1.2 Opening Microsoft Word

Microsoft Word is a popular word processing program that's accessible to users of Windows 10 and 11. Here are a few easy steps to get started with Microsoft Word on Windows 10 and 11:

- Open the Windows Start menu by clicking on it at the bottom left of the screen or pressing the Windows key on your keyboard.
- Enter "Microsoft Word" into the search bar.
- Click on the Microsoft Word application icon in the search results.
- You can also locate Microsoft Word in the list of installed apps in the Start menu.
- After opening the Microsoft Word application, you can either start new documents or access existing

ones by choosing the relevant options from the menu.

You also have the option of pinning Microsoft Word to your taskbar, making it easily accessible whenever you need it in the future.

1.3 Searching for Microsoft Word

Looking for Microsoft Word? No worries, I've got you covered! There are a couple of ways to find it.

- To find Microsoft Word, start by clicking on the Start menu. Then, enter "Microsoft Word" into the search bar. Look for the suggestion in the Word app icon, then click on it to open the program.
- You can also use File Explorer to find Microsoft Word. Simply click on the folder icon in the taskbar or press Windows key + E to open File Explorer. Then, enter "Microsoft Word" into the search bar, and choose the appropriate result.

1.4 Pin Microsoft Word to Your Taskbar

Here's how you can easily pin Microsoft Word to your taskbar for quick access:

- On your computer, open Microsoft Word.
- Once the program is open, right-click on its icon in the taskbar.
- From the context menu that appears, select "Pin to taskbar."
- Microsoft Word will now be pinned to your taskbar, allowing you to launch it with just a single click whenever you need it.

After closing Microsoft Word, its icon remains on the taskbar. This convenient feature eliminates the need for you to search for it every time you want to use it again.

Chapter 2: An Overview of Microsoft Word

2.1 Definition of Microsoft Word: What Is It? Why does Microsoft Word get used?

Curious about Microsoft Word and its uses? For creative professionals, understanding Microsoft Word can be valuable—it's a tool that makes crafting impressive documents easy.

Let's dig into MS Word. Here, I'll explain, "What is Microsoft Word, and what do people use it for?" We'll look at its main features and assist you in getting started. Soon, you'll grasp the basics of Microsoft Word and its functionalities!

2.1.1 What is Microsoft Word?

What exactly is Microsoft Word? It's a word processor, which means it's an app for handling text-based documents. With it, you can format, save, edit, print, and share your documents seamlessly.

Let's talk about Microsoft Word. It's among the most widely used word processors globally and is part of the Microsoft 365 suite of productivity tools. If you've used PowerPoint, Outlook, or Excel, you're already acquainted with Microsoft 365 applications.

Microsoft Word is accessible on Windows, Mac, and various mobile devices. Additionally, there's a free web-based version that works in your browser, making it a solid choice for those new to Microsoft Word.

2.2 How to Use Microsoft Word for the First Time

What's your familiarity with Microsoft Word? It's alright if your answer is "very little." I'll provide you with helpful tips to get you started on understanding Microsoft Word.

At first, starting with Microsoft Word as a beginner may seem overwhelming. However, the application has become more user-friendly over time, catering to users of all expertise levels. So, what exactly is Microsoft Word used for, and how can you begin using it?

What stands out as Microsoft Word's most crucial feature? There are so many to choose from! Let's explore some of the essential ones together.

2.2.1 Navigating the Microsoft Word Interface

Microsoft Word is a versatile word processing tool. To use it effectively, you need to become familiar with its user interface and primary menus. Fortunately, these elements remain consistent across different versions of Word.

At the top of the Word window, you'll see the ribbon. This section houses the essential menu tabs you'll frequently use. They're clearly labeled as:

- Home
- Insert
- Draw
- Design
- Layout
- References
- Mailings
- Review
- View

At the top of your screen, you'll notice the main menu, which includes important options such as:

- File
- Edit
- View
- Insert
- Format
- Tools
- Table
- Window
- Help

When you click on any of these options, you'll see the menu items change accordingly. This is where you'll find most of Microsoft Word's editing features.

There are some features that are common between the menu and the ribbon tabs. However, you can think of the ribbon as the place where you'll manage your document's appearance. On the other hand, the menu tabs are there to help you with sharing, printing, and managing Word's functions.

Take a moment to explore these tabs and their options. Chances are, you will find the tools you want on the ribbon. For instance, let's take a peek at the ribbon's Insert tab. Here, you'll find buttons to add links, page numbers, images, and other elements.

2.3 An Extensive Examination of the Microsoft Word Interface

The first time you open Word, you'll see the Start Screen. It lets you start a new document, pick a template, or open recent documents. To get to the Word interface, just choose "Blank document" from the Start Screen.

In the latest versions, Word still uses familiar tools like the Ribbon, Quick Access Toolbar (with common commands), and Backstage View.

2.3.1 The Ribbon

Instead of traditional menus, Word uses a tabbed ribbon system. This ribbon has several tabs located at the top of the Microsoft Word window. Each tab in Word includes various groups of common commands. For instance, on the Home tab, you'll find the Font group with options for text formatting in your document. Certain groups also feature a little arrow in the lower-right corner, which you can click to access additional options.

2.3.2 Displaying and Concealing the Ribbon

To free up screen space, you can hide the ribbon in Word. Simply click the arrow in the top-right corner of your ribbon, then choose the option you would like from the drop-down menu:

2.3.2.1 Auto-Hide Ribbon

When you choose auto-hide, your document fills the screen entirely, hiding the ribbon. To bring back the ribbon, click on the Expand Ribbon command located at the top of your screen.

2.3.2.2 Show Tabs

Choosing this option hides every command group when they're not being used, keeping only the tabs visible. To bring back the ribbon, just click on any tab.

2.3.2.3 Show Tabs and Commands

When you choose this option, the ribbon is fully displayed, with every tab and command visible. It's the default setting when you first open Word.

2.3.3 Making Use of the "Tell Me" Feature

If you have trouble finding a command, you can use the Tell Me feature. It's like a search bar: just enter what you need, and options will show up. Then, you can use the command right from the menu without searching through the ribbon.

2.3.4 Using the Quick Access Toolbar

Right on top of the ribbon, you'll find the Quick Access Toolbar. It gives you quick access to similar commands, no matter which tab you're on. It starts with the Redo, Undo, and Save commands but can be customized with other commands you use frequently.

To put commands on the Quick Access Toolbar:

- Click on the arrow to the right-side of the Quick Access Toolbar.

- Click on the command you would like to include from the menu.
- The command you selected will now appear on the Quick Access Toolbar.

2.3.5 Making Use of the Ruler

You'll find the Ruler at the left and top of your Word document, helping you make precise adjustments. If needed, you can conceal the ruler to free up extra screen space.

2.3.5.1 Displaying and Concealing the Ruler

To display or hide the ruler,

- Go to the View tab.
- Check or uncheck the box beside the ruler to display or conceal the ruler.

2.3.6 Accessing the Backstage View

The Backstage View in Microsoft Word is where you can manage your document as a whole. It's where you go to perform tasks like saving, printing, and sharing your document.

- To access the Backstage View, you simply need to click on the "File" tab at the top left corner of the Word window.
- Once you click on the "File" tab, you'll see the Backstage View appear. From there, you can find options for saving your document, printing it, sharing it with others, and more.

It's a convenient hub for managing your document and accessing essential functions in Word.

2.3.7 Zooming and Changing the Views of Your Documents

In Microsoft Word, there are different ways to view your document. You can use Read Mode, Web Layout, or Print Layout, each offering a distinct display style. These options come in handy, especially when preparing to print your document. Additionally, you can zoom in or out to adjust the document's readability as needed.

2.3.8 Flipping Between Different Document Views

Navigating through various document views in Word is simple. You can do this by searching for and clicking on the specific command for the document view you want, located in the lower-right corner of your Word window.

2.3.8.1 Read Mode

This particular view enlarges the document to occupy the entire screen, which is especially useful for reading extensive text or reviewing your content.

2.3.8.2 Print Layout

This default view in Microsoft Word displays the document as it would appear when printed on paper.

2.3.8.3 Web Layout

This view presents the document in a format resembling a webpage, which would be advantageous if you intend to use Microsoft Word to publish content on the internet.

2.3.9 Zooming in and out

You can adjust the zoom level in Word by clicking and dragging the zoom control slider located at the lower-right corner of your window. Alternatively, you can use the "+" and "-" commands for smaller zoom adjustments. The number beside the slider indicates the current zoom level, also known as the zoom percentage.

2.3.10 Adjusting the Text's Size

Keyboard shortcuts are the quickest way to resize text. Here's a straightforward way to adjust text size:

- To highlight the text you'd like to resize, select it.
- Hold down the "Ctrl" key on your keyboard and press the "]" button to increase the font size. Alternatively, press "Ctrl" and "[" to decrease the size of your text.
- Repeat using the "Ctrl" and "]" or "[" keys until you reach the desired text size.

Here's a handy tip: while holding down the "Ctrl" key, you can also make use of the mouse wheel to swiftly adjust your text size.

2.4 Exiting Word

Closing Microsoft Word is simple.

If you're using a computer, look for the small "X" in the top-right corner of the window, then click it. Alternatively, you can press the "Alt" key on your keyboard and then press the "F4" button to close the program.

On a Mac, you'll find the "X" in the top-left corner, and you can also use the "Cmd" and "Q" keys as a shortcut to exit. These methods ensure you can quickly and efficiently close Microsoft Word whenever you're done working.

Chapter 3: Input Devices Set Up

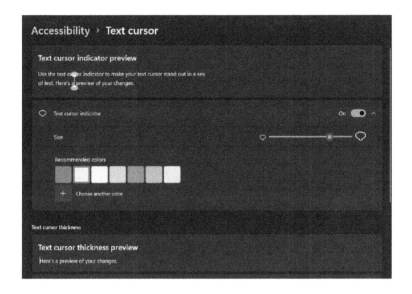

3.1 Make Using Your Computer's Mouse, Keyboard, and Other Input Devices More Convenient

You can enhance the usability of your computer peripherals, such as the keyboard or mouse, in various ways.

3.2 The Mouse

Simplifying mouse usage for improved usability. Here's how:

3.2.1 Make Changes to the Main Mouse Button, Show Pointer Traces, or Configure Scrolling Parameters

- To access your computer's settings, press the Windows logo key along with the letter "I" or click on Start, then Settings.

- Next, choose Bluetooth and devices, and then click on Mouse.

  a) To switch the primary mouse button, expand the menu labeled Primary Mouse Button and choose your preferred option from the list.

  b) Choose the appropriate scrolling options by selecting the desired settings under the Scrolling section.

  c) To make your cursor leave a trail as you move it on the screen, follow these steps: Go to Additional Mouse Settings, then click on the Pointer Options tab, and finally, check the box labeled Display pointer trails.

3.2.2 Using a Numeric Keypad to Control the Mouse

- To access your computer's accessibility settings, either press the Windows logo key along with the letter "U" or click on Start, then Settings, followed by Accessibility.

- Next, navigate to the mouse option under Interaction.
- Activate the Mouse Keys option by toggling the switch to the "on" position.

3.2.3 Increasing Your Mouse Cursor's Visibility

By enlarging or altering the color of your mouse pointer, you can improve its visibility.

- To access your computer's accessibility settings, either press the Windows logo key along with the letter "U" or click on Start, then Settings, and finally Accessibility.
- Next, click on the mouse pointer and touch.
- To resize your mouse pointer, move the size slider under Mouse Pointer until it reaches your preferred size.
- Next, choose a mouse pointer style option to change the color to black, white, inverted, or one of the recommended bright colors. For further customization, click on Choose Another Color.

3.3 The Text Cursor: Improving Visibility

In Windows 11, you can adjust the text cursor thickness and add a colorful indicator to improve the text cursor's visibility.

3.3.1 Make Use of the Text Cursor Indicator

- To access your computer's accessibility settings, press the Windows logo key along with the letter "U" or click on Start, then Settings, and then Accessibility.
- Once there, choose the text cursor.
- Activate the text cursor indicator by toggling the switch to the "on" position.
- Then, use the Size slider to adjust the indicator's size until it matches your preference in the preview.
- To adjust the indicator color, pick one from the Recommended Colors list or click on Choose Another Color to select a custom color of your choice.

3.3.2 Modifying the Thickness of the Text Cursor

- To access your computer's accessibility settings, press the Windows logo key along with the letter "U" or click on Start, then Settings, and finally Accessibility.
- From there, click on Text cursor to select it.

- To change the thickness of the text cursor, use the text cursor thickness slider to adjust the thickness until it appears as you prefer in the preview.

3.4 Make Working on the Keyboard More Convenient

- To access your computer's accessibility settings, press the Windows logo key along with the letter "U" or click on Start, then Settings, and select Accessibility.
- From there, choose Keyboard and explore some of the available options:

a) Activate the Sticky Keys option if you find it difficult to press two keys simultaneously. Sticky keys allow you to input commands that require multiple keys, like Ctrl + S, by pressing each key individually.

b) Enable the on-screen keyboard switch to choose keys using a mouse or any other pointing device, such as a joystick, or to cycle through the keys on the screen using a single switch.

c) Enable the Filter keys option to adjust the keyboard sensitivity, allowing it to disregard short or repeated keystrokes.

d) Activate the toggle keys option to hear a sound each time you press the scroll lock, num lock, or cap lock keys.

e) Enable the option to use the Print Screen button for screen snipping by toggling the switch to the "on" position.

f) Activate the Underline Access Keys option to have access keys underlined when they are available.

3.5 Setting Up Input Devices on a Mac

Adjusting some settings on your Mac can enhance your typing experience when using Microsoft Word. Here's how:

3.6 Using your Mac's Keyboard as a Mouse

Your keyboard can do more than just type. It can also help you navigate through items, lists, text boxes, icons, and menus on your computer. When navigating, use the Tab key to move forward and Shift + Tab to move backward.

- To access keyboard settings on your Mac, click on the Apple menu, then go to System Settings, and select Keyboard from the sidebar (you might need to scroll down to find it).

- Enable "keyboard navigation" by clicking on it. Once activated, you can use the Tab key to move to the next control on your screen and Shift-Tab to move to the previous one.

To limit tab-key navigation to lists and text boxes only, disable "keyboard navigation."

3.7 Toggle the Backlighting on Your Mac Keyboard On and Off

If your Mac computer comes with a backlit keyboard, you have the option to adjust the backlight manually or opt for automatic settings to control it.

3.7.1 Automatically Adjusting Your Keyboard Backlighting

Your Mac can automatically adjust the keyboard backlight in low light and can also turn off the backlight after a period of inactivity. Here are the steps:

3.7.1.1 Automatically Turning Off Your Keyboard Backlight After a Time of Inactivity

Here are the steps to follow:

- Go to the Apple menu and select System Settings. Then, click on Keyboard in the sidebar.
- On the right side, locate the "Turn keyboard backlight off after inactivity" option. Click on the pop-up menu next to it and choose a time duration from the available options.

Remember to keep the area close to your computer's camera unobstructed, especially in low-light environments, as this is where the light sensor is located.

3.7.1.2 Automatically Adjusting Keyboard Backlight in Low Light Situations

- Navigate to the Apple menu and select System Settings. Then, click on Keyboard in the sidebar.
- On the right-hand side, enable the option "Adjust keyboard brightness in low light."

3.7.2 Manually Changing or Disabling the Keyboard Backlighting

Choose one of these options:

3.7.2.1 Mac Computers with Touch Bars

- For Macs equipped with a Touch Bar, expand the Control Strip and tap the increase brightness button to make it brighter or the decrease brightness button to dim it.
- Hold down the decrease brightness button to switch off the backlighting.

3.7.2.2 Mac Computers with Keyboard Brightness Keys

- If your Mac includes dedicated keyboard brightness keys, you can adjust the brightness by pressing the increase or decrease brightness keys.
- To switch off your keyboard's backlighting, simply continue to press the decrease brightness key until it is off.

3.7.2.3 Every Mac Computer

To adjust the keyboard brightness on your Mac:

- Click on the Apple menu, then select System Preferences, followed by Keyboard in the sidebar (you might need to scroll down).
- On the right side, use the keyboard-brightness slider to modify the brightness level. Sliding the brightness control to the far left will switch off the backlighting.

3.7.2.4 Adjusting Keyboard Brightness from Your Desktop

To change the keyboard brightness straight from your desktop, you can add the Keyboard Brightness module to the Control Center or the menu bar. Here's how:

- Click on the Apple menu, then go to System Preferences, and select Control Center from the sidebar (you may need to scroll down to find it).
- On the right side, locate Keyboard Brightness and toggle "Show in Menu Bar" or "Show in Control Center."
- To modify the brightness, click on the Keyboard Brightness icon in the Control Center or menu bar.

3.8 Modify How Quickly the Mac Keyboard Responds

You can change the delay between pressing a key on your Mac's keyboard and when it responds if you find that it's too quick for your liking.

To adjust the delay between pressing keys and your Mac's response, follow these steps:

- Open the Apple menu, go to System Settings, then select Accessibility in the sidebar, and select Keyboard.
- Once in the keyboard settings, enable "Slow Keys" by ticking the checkbox next to it. You can learn more about Slow Keys by clicking the Info button.
- Adjust the "Acceptance delay" slider to determine the delay time before your Mac responds after you press a key.

If you want an audible feedback sound with each keystroke response, enable "Use click key sounds."

3.9 Adjust the Speed at Which a Key Repeats on MacOS

When you hold down specific keys on your keyboard while typing, the character associated with that key will start repeating. For instance, if you press and hold the Delete key while in a text area, it will continue to erase text as long as you keep it pressed.

You have the option to adjust the duration of time you need to hold a key before it begins to repeat, as well as how quickly it repeats once it does start.

- To access keyboard settings on your Mac, start by clicking on the Apple menu, then select System Settings. From there, navigate to the keyboard option in the sidebar.
- On the keyboard settings page, adjust how your Mac responds to keypresses.

    a) Use the "Delay until repeat" slider to set the time before a character starts repeating after holding a key.

    b) Use the "Key repeat rate" slider to adjust how quickly characters repeat when a key is held down.

Chapter 4: Editing a Microsoft Word Document

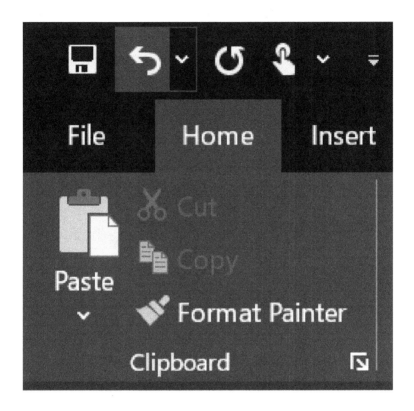

4.1 Removing Text from a Word Document

If you need to remove characters, words, or entire lines of text from your document, there are multiple methods available. The following topics discuss different ways to delete text from your document.

4.1.1 Deleting a Character or a Number of Characters

To delete specific characters (symbols, numbers, or letters) in a document using Microsoft Word, follow these steps:

- Open your document in Microsoft Word.
- Position the mouse cursor just after the last character you would like to remove.
- Left-click your mouse to position the cursor after the last character.
- Push the Backspace key once or multiple times to remove the characters preceding the cursor.

As an alternative,

- Start by opening your document in Microsoft Word.
- Then, place your mouse cursor on the first character you wish to remove.
- Left-click your mouse to position the cursor in front of the first character.
- Then, hit the Delete key once or several times to remove the characters that come after the cursor.

Note: If you're using an Apple keyboard that lacks a Backspace key and only has a Delete key, pressing Delete will remove the text in front of the cursor instead.

4.1.2 Deleting an Entire Word

To delete a whole word in a document using Microsoft Word, follow these steps:

- Begin by opening your Microsoft Word document.
- Then, position the mouse cursor at the start of the specific word you wish to delete.
- Hold down the left mouse button and drag the mouse to the right-side to highlight the whole word.
- After the word is highlighted, hit the Delete or Backspace key to delete it.

Alternatively,

- Start by opening the Microsoft Word document.
- Then, place your mouse cursor on the specific word you wish to delete.
- Double-click with the left mouse button to select the whole word.
- Then, hit the Delete or Backspace key to remove the word.

A helpful tip: To select a whole word using only your keyboard, simply press and hold down the Shift and Ctrl keys simultaneously. Then, press the arrow key in the desired direction to highlight the word.

Note: If you're using an Apple keyboard that lacks a Backspace key and only has a Delete key, pressing the Delete key will delete the text in front of the cursor.

4.1.3 Deleting an Entire Line of Text

To delete a whole line of text in Microsoft Word, follow these steps:

- First, open your document.
- Then, position the mouse cursor at the start of the specific line of text you intend to remove.
- Hold down the left mouse button and drag your mouse to the right-side until the whole line of text is selected.
- After the line of text is highlighted, hit the Delete or Backspace key to remove it.

On the other hand,

- Start by opening your document.
- Next, position your cursor to the left-side of the text line you wish to remove, specifically in the margin area. You should see the cursor shaped like a right-slanting arrow.
- Left-click your mouse to select the whole line of text.
- Then, hit the Delete or Backspace key to remove the whole line of text.

Here's a helpful tip: Hold down the Shift key and use the down arrow or up arrow key to select a row of text per time. Another method is to hold down the Shift key and use the Page Up or Down keys to select a page of text at a time. After highlighting the text, you can delete it by pressing the Delete or Backspace key.

Note: On Apple keyboards that do not have a Backspace key but have a Delete key, pressing Delete will remove the text in front of the cursor.

4.1.4 Deleting All Text from a Word Document

To remove all text from a Word document, use the keyboard shortcut Ctrl+A on Windows or Command+A on MacOS to select all text. After highlighting all the text, press the Delete or Backspace key to erase it.

4.2 Splitting and Joining Paragraphs

Splitting and joining paragraphs in Microsoft Word is quite straightforward. Here's how:

4.2.1 Split a Paragraph

- Open Microsoft Word and navigate to the document you wish to edit.
- Locate the paragraph you intend to split.
- To split a paragraph, position your cursor at the point where you want to split the paragraph.
- Then, press the Enter key on your keyboard.

This action will create a new paragraph starting from the cursor's position.

On the other hand, here's how to join a paragraph:

4.2.2 Join a Paragraph

- Open Microsoft Word and navigate to the document you wish to edit.
- Locate the paragraphs you intend to join.
- If you wish to join two paragraphs into one, place your cursor at the end of the first paragraph.
- Next, press the Delete key to remove any extra spaces or line breaks between the paragraphs.

This will seamlessly merge the two paragraphs into a single paragraph.

4.3 Hard Return: What is it?

A hard return is a term used to describe the action of inserting a line break in a text or document. This is achieved by pressing the Enter key on the keyboard, which visibly moves the text or cursor to the next line.

4.3.1 What Applications Do Hard Returns Serve?

In word processing applications such as Microsoft Word, hard returns are frequently employed to make paragraphs, divide lines of text, or organize content in an aesthetically pleasing manner.

4.3.2 What Distinguishes a Soft Return from a Hard Return?

When you use a hard return, it creates a noticeable line break in your text. In contrast, a soft return creates a line break without initiating a new paragraph. In Microsoft Word, you can generate a soft return by pushing the Shift + Enter keys on the keyboard. Soft returns come in handy when you need to break a line of text without introducing additional spacing between the paragraphs.

4.4 Undoing, Redoing, and Repeating a Microsoft Word Action on Windows

In Microsoft Word, there are several ways to backtrack or repeat actions you've taken. You can undo changes even after saving your document, and then save it again. By default, Microsoft Office retains the last hundred actions that can be undone.

4.4.1 The Undo Command

To reverse an action in Microsoft Word, you can use the keyboard shortcut Ctrl+Z or click on the Undo option in the Quick Access Toolbar. If you need to undo several steps, simply press Ctrl+Z or click Undo numerous times.

Certain actions in Microsoft Word cannot be undone, like choosing options from the File tab or saving a file. When an action cannot be undone, the Undo command will switch to "Can't Undo."

To reverse multiple actions simultaneously in Microsoft Word, click on the arrow beside the Undo button. From the list that appears, choose the specific actions you intend to undo, and then click on the list.

4.4.2 The Redo Command

To redo an action that you've undone in Microsoft Word, you can use the keyboard shortcuts Ctrl+Y or F4. If F4 does not work, try pressing the Fn or F-Lock key first while holding down the F4 key simultaneously. Alternatively, you can click on the Redo option in the Quick Access toolbar, which only becomes available after you have undone an action.

4.4.3 The Repeat Command

To repeat a straightforward action like pasting, you can use the keyboard shortcuts Ctrl+Y or F4. If F4 does not work initially, try pressing the Fn or F-Lock key first while simultaneously holding down the F4 key. Alternatively, you can click on the Repeat option in the Quick Access Toolbar.

Keep in mind that certain actions, like utilizing a function within an Excel cell, cannot be redone. When you're unable to repeat the previous action, the Repeat command will change to "Can't Repeat."

4.5 Undoing, Redoing, and Repeating a Microsoft Word Action on MacOS

The following are methods to undo, redo, and repeat actions in Microsoft Word on MacOS:

4.5.1 The Undo Command

To undo an action in Microsoft Word on MacOS, you can use the keyboard shortcut Command + Z or click the Undo option from the top-left corner of your ribbon until the problem is corrected.

Certain actions, like saving a file or choosing commands from the File menu, cannot be undone in Microsoft Word. When an action is not undoable, the Undo command will change to "Can't Undo."

To reverse multiple actions simultaneously in Microsoft Word, click on the arrow beside the Undo command, choose the actions you would like to undo from the list, and then click on the list.

4.5.2 The Redo Command

To redo an action you have undone in Microsoft Word on MacOS, use the keyboard shortcut Command + Y or click Redo on the top-left corner of the ribbon. Remember, the redo button will only show up after an action has been undone.

4.5.3 The Repeat Command

To repeat a simple action, like pasting in Microsoft Word on MacOS, use the keyboard shortcut Command + Y or click Repeat on the top-left corner of the ribbon.

Chapter 5: Formatting Your Word Document

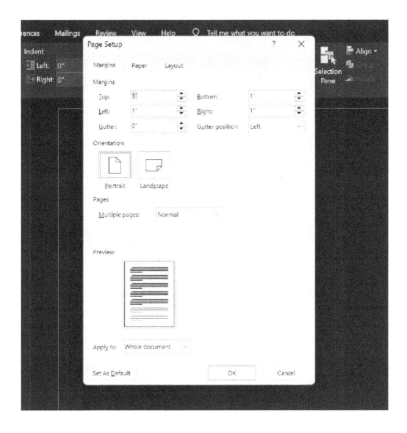

5.1 Customizing or Crafting Your Own Styles

Styles in Word allow you to apply consistent formatting across your document with efficiency. If the built-in themes and styles don't offer the specific formatting you need, you can adjust an existing style to match your requirements. This includes modifying text indentation, color, font size, and more for lists, paragraphs, headings, titles, and other elements. Additionally, you can create a new style based on formatted text within your document using the Styles gallery.

In this chapter, you'll find the styles mentioned listed in the Styles gallery, which is a visual menu found on the Home tab. To use a style, just choose the text you want to format and then click on the desired style from the Styles gallery.

5.2 Tweaking a Style That's Already There

You can change an existing style in the Styles gallery using two methods:

a) Updating a style to match the formatting in your Word document.

b) Changing a style manually using the Modify Style dialog box.

5.2.1 Updating a Style to Match Your Word Document's Formatting

If there's text in your Word document with an existing style, you can modify its formatting and then apply it to the style in your Styles gallery.

- Choose the text in your Word document that already uses an applied style, such as "Heading 1." When you highlight such text, the corresponding style gets highlighted in your Styles gallery as well.
- Next, apply the desired changes to the selected text. For instance, you could adjust the Heading 1 style's font size from 14 points to 12 points.
- Go to the Home tab, then locate the Styles group. Right-click on the style you intend to modify. Choose "Update [Style Name] to Match Selection." Remember, every text with that style will automatically update to match your changes.

5.2.2 Manually Adjusting a Style Using the Modify Style Dialog Box

You have the option to adjust a style directly within the Styles gallery without needing to edit the text in your Microsoft Word document.

- To tweak a style, head to the Home tab, right-click on any style within the Styles gallery, and select Modify.
- Under the Formatting section, apply any changes you wish, like adjusting the indentation, line spacing, or alignment, altering color, font size, or font style.
- Decide if the style adjustments should affect only this document or every future one.

5.3 Generating a New Style Using the Current Document's Formatting as a Base

You can choose the text in your document with the desired formatting to establish a new style for inclusion in the Styles gallery.

- Simply right-click on the text that serves as the foundation for the new style you wish to create.
- In the small toolbar that pops up, select Styles, and then choose Create a Style.
- In the window for creating a new style from formatting, name the new style, and then click OK to apply changes.

The style you've created will now show up in the Styles gallery for easy access.

Note: To have your new style apply to every new Word document, right-click on the style in the Styles gallery, choose Modify, and then opt for "New documents based on this template," located at the lower part of the dialog box.

5.4 Setting Up Your Document Using Word Headings

Headings help readers grasp important information quickly. Learn how to apply styles to headings in your Word documents to improve their navigability.

5.4.1 Adding a Heading Style

To include a heading style in your Word document:

- In your Word document, enter the desired text.
- Pick out the sentence you wish to turn into a header by highlighting it.
- Go to the Home tab, click on Styles (or use the keyboard shortcut Alt+H, then press the L key), and choose the desired heading style, like the Heading 1 button.

In Microsoft Word, a title is formatted with a font and color change to indicate it's Heading 1 of the article. Heading 2 is the following heading type.

5.5 Changing, Customizing, and Saving a Theme

In Word documents, the default color theme palette includes shades of gray, yellow, orange, green, and blue, but it doesn't have purple or red. While you can still use other colors, this palette determines the choices available for tables, SmartArt, and charts.

Knowing how to adjust the color palette can improve your workflow and ensure a uniform visual appearance.

5.5.1 Accessing the Color Palettes Menu

To open the color palette menu in Microsoft Word, follow these steps:

- Start a Word document.
- Locate and click on the Design tab.
- Next, click on the Colors menu located to the right and choose a palette with various color choices. A commonly used palette is the Office 2007–2010 option.

5.5.2 Working with Themes and Making Adjustments

Themes are collections of font styles and colors that you can apply to a document. The default theme is usually "Office," but you have the option to use other themes. Additionally, you can customize colors and fonts according to your preferences.

5.5.2.1 Updating Themes

To change the theme in Word, follow these steps:

- Open a Microsoft Word document and navigate to the Design tab.
- From the Themes menu located on the left side, choose a theme that you prefer.
- Make use of the Colors and Fonts menus that appear on the right side to make any necessary formatting changes.

5.5.2.2 Saving and Reusing a Custom Theme

- After adjusting the colors and fonts to your liking, go to the theme menu.

- Then, choose "Save Current Theme," located at the lower part of the menu. This action will open a save window.
- After naming and saving your ".thmx" theme file, proceed to open a new Word document.
- Next, navigate to the theme menu within the Design tab. You will find your saved theme listed under the Custom options.

5.5.3 Choosing a New Default Theme

If you want a different theme to be the default instead of the Office theme, you can set your preferred theme in the following way:

- Start by opening a Word document.
- Then, go to the Design tab, where you can choose and personalize your preferred theme. If necessary, save any customized theme.
- In the Design tab, click on "Set as Default," positioned to the right-side of the Colors and Fonts menu.
- A new window will appear; choose "Yes" if you wish for this theme to be the default for future documents.

5.5.4 Modify, Save, and Use a Theme in Word on MacOS

Themes in Office offer comprehensive designs for your Word document, encompassing layouts, colors, font choices, and background styles. You have the flexibility to customize these themes provided by Office and save them for repeated use.

- If you have not chosen a theme yet, go to the Design tab, click on Themes, and select the one you prefer.
- Customize the theme according to your preferences by adjusting page borders, background colors, watermarks, paragraph spacing, fonts, or colors on the Design tab.
- Navigate to the Design tab, then select Themes and choose Save Current Theme.
- Enter a name for the new theme in the Save Current Theme dialog box and click Save to apply changes.
- To use your theme in a different document, go to the Design tab, click on Themes, and choose your theme from the Custom section.

5.6 Setting Up Your Page Layout

In Word, there are many options for arranging and formatting pages, which impact how content is displayed. You can adjust the margins, paper size, and page orientation to suit the desired look of your Word document.

5.6.1 Page Orientation

In Microsoft Word, you have two page orientation choices: portrait and landscape. The difference lies in how the page is oriented, either horizontally (landscape) or vertically (portrait). This orientation affects how text and images are displayed and spaced on the page.

5.6.1.1 Changing the Page Orientation

To change the page orientation:

- Go to the Layout tab and click it.
- Click on the orientation option located in the Page Setup group.
- You will see a drop-down menu. Click on either landscape or portrait to switch the page orientation.

This action will adjust the document's page orientation accordingly.

5.6.2 Page Margins

A margin refers to the distance between the edges of your document and the text. When you start a new document, the margins are typically set to Normal, giving you a 1-inch space around the text. However, in Word, you have the flexibility to adjust the margin size according to your requirements.

5.6.2.1 Formatting Page Margins

In Word, you'll find several pre-set margin sizes available for selection.

- First, go to the Layout tab, and then click on Margins.
- You'll see a drop-down menu where you can choose from various pre-set margin sizes. Simply click on the one that suits your needs.
- After selecting a new margin size, your document's margins will be updated accordingly.

5.6.2.2 Using a Custom Margin

In Word, you have the option to personalize the margin size through the Page Setup dialog box.

- Click on the Margins option within the Layout tab.
- From there, choose Custom Margins. This action will open the Page Setup dialog box.
- Next, modify the numerical values for each margin as needed in the Page Setup dialog box.
- Once you're done, click OK to apply the changes, and your document's margins will be updated accordingly.

Alternatively, to access the Page Setup dialog box, go to the Layout tab and click the small arrow located in the lower-right corner of the Page Setup group.

5.6.3 Page Size

When you start a new document, it typically comes with a default page size of 8.5 inches by 11 inches. However, depending on the type of project you are working on, you might want to change this size. Before doing so, make sure to check what page sizes your printer can handle.

5.6.3.1 Adjusting the Page Size

In Word, there are several preset page sizes available for selection.

- Navigate to the Layout tab and click on Size.
- A drop-down menu will show the current page size highlighted. Simply choose the preferred preset page size from the options provided.
- Once you select a new page size, the document's page size will be updated accordingly.

5.6.3.2 Setting a Custom Page Size

You can also adjust the page size to your preference using the Page Setup dialog box in Word.

- First, go to the Layout tab and click on Size.
- Then, choose More Paper Sizes from the drop-down menu. This action will open the Page Setup dialog box.
- In the Page Setup dialog box, you can adjust the values for width and height according to your preferences.
- Once you're done, click OK to apply the changes, and the page size of your document will be updated accordingly.

5.7 Page Breaks

In Word, a new page break is automatically inserted at the end of every page. However, you can also manually insert a page break whenever you wish to begin a new page in the Word document.

5.7.1 Inserting a Page Break in Your Document on Windows

- First, place your mouse cursor in the position where you would like one page to end and the next one to start.
- Then, navigate to the Insert tab and click on Page Break.

5.7.2 Adding a Manual Page Break on MacOS

- To insert a page break in your document, tap or click on the position where you would like the break.
- Then, go to the Layout tab, click on Breaks, and select Page.

5.7.3 Adding a Page Break in Web Versions

- To add a page break to your document, click or tap where you want it.
- Then, go to the Insert tab and select Page Break.

5.8 Removing a Manual Page Break

If you ever need to eliminate page breaks from your document, follow these steps:

5.8.1 Deleting a Page Break on Windows

- To view page breaks while working on your document, click on the Show/Hide icon in the Home tab.
  Note: The "show/hide" icon in Microsoft Word is typically represented by a paragraph symbol (¶). It appears as a small, backward-facing "P" in Word's toolbar or ribbon.
- Once the page breaks are visible, double-click on the specific page break that you want to remove to highlight it.
- Then, hit the Delete key on your keyboard to remove it.

5.8.2 Deleting a Page Break on MacOS

- To show page breaks as you work on your document, click the Show/Hide icon in the Home tab. This will reveal the page breaks.
- Then, position your cursor just after the paragraph mark in the desired page break, and hit the Delete key on your keyboard to remove it.

5.8.3 Deleting a Page Break on the Web

In Editing View on Word for the web, a page break that was manually inserted will appear as a visible line that separates the pages. However, it won't be visible in Reading View.

To remove a page break in Word for the web, follow these steps:

- If you are not already in Editing View, choose "Edit Document" and then "Edit in Word for the web."
- Select the specific page break that you want to delete.
- Press the Delete key on your keyboard. This process will eliminate the selected page break from your document.

Please keep in mind that you can only remove the page breaks that you manually inserted in your documents. The page break that Word automatically adds as text flows from one page to another cannot be deleted.

5.9 Inserting a Section Break on Windows

Use section breaks to effectively organize and format documents, regardless of their size. For instance, you can segment documents into chapters and apply various formatting elements like page borders, headers, footers, and columns to each section as needed.

To insert a section break, follow these steps:

- Choose the location where you would like the new section to start.
- Navigate to the Layout tab and click on Breaks.
- Select the type of section break based on your needs:

a) "Next Page": This type of section break begins the new section on the next page.

b) "Continuous": This section break begins the new section on the same page. It's commonly used to adjust column numbers without creating a new page.

c) "Even Page": This section break initiates a new section on the following page that has an even page number.

d) "Odd Page": This type of section break begins a new section on the following page with an odd page number.

5.10 Adding a Section Break on MacOS

To start a new section in your document, follow these steps:

- Choose the location where you would like the new section to start.
- Navigate to the Layout tab, click on Breaks, and select the type of section break you need.

a) "Next Page": This option begins the new section on the page that follows.

b) "Continuous": This type of section break begins the new section on the same page. It's handy for documents with columns, allowing you to adjust the column layout without creating a new page.

c) "Even Page": This type of section break begins the new section on the following page with an even page number. For instance, if you decide to add an even page break to the end of page 4, the following section will begin on page 5.

d) "Odd Page": This section break begins the new section on the following page with an odd page number. For instance, if you choose to add an Odd Page Section Break to the end of page 4, the next section will begin on page 6.

5.11 Working with Headers or Footers
Here's how to add a header or footer in Microsoft Word on both Windows and Mac computers:

5.11.1 Adding a Header or Footer on Windows
To insert a header or footer in Microsoft Word, follow these steps:

- Click on Insert, then select Header or Footer.
- Select the header style that suits your needs. Note that some built-in designs include page numbers within the header or footer.
- To add or edit text in the header or footer, double-click on the existing header or footer to enter editing mode.
- Make the necessary changes or additions to the text as required.

5.11.2 Removing a Header from the Title Page

To remove a header, such as from the title page, follow these steps:

- Select the header area.
- Check the box labeled "Different First Page."
- Click on "Close Header and Footer" or hit the Esc key on your keyboard to exit.

5.11.3 Deleting a Header or Footer

To delete a header or footer, follow these steps:

- Click on Insert, then select "Header" (or "Footer").
- Choose "Remove Header" (or "Remove Footer") from the options provided.

5.11.4 Inserting a Standard or Custom Header or Footer on MacOS

Here's how to add a standard or custom header or footer on a Mac computer:

- Click Insert, then choose Header or Footer.
- From the header or footer options, select the desired standard header or footer from the list provided.

- Alternatively, you can create a customized header or footer by choosing "Edit Header" or "Edit Footer."
- Once you've finished editing, click on "Close Header and Footer" or use the Esc key on your keyboard.

5.12 Adding or Removing Page Numbers in a Word Document

Here's how you can add or remove basic page numbering in your document:

5.12.1 Inserting Page Numbers

Here are the steps to add page numbers in Word:

- Go to the Insert tab, then select Page Number.
- Choose the location where you intend to display the page number.
- Select your preferred style, and Word will automatically add page numbers to each page for you.

5.12.2 Begin Page Numbering from the Second Page

- To adjust the page numbering format, first double-click inside the header or footer area to open the Header & Footer Tools.
- Then, go to the Design tab, click on Page Number, and choose Format Page Numbers.
- Set the "Start at" option to 0 and click OK. Then, choose "Different First Page," followed by clicking on "Close Header and Footer."

5.12.3 Removing Page Numbers

To remove page numbers from your document, follow these steps:

- Click Insert, then go to Page Number.
- Choose the option "Remove Page Numbers."

5.13 Automatic Table of Contents

Creating a table of contents in Microsoft Word relies on the headings used in your document. Here's how to insert one:

5.13.1 Creating Table of Contents on Windows

- Position the cursor where you would like the table of contents to appear.
- Navigate to the References tab, then click on the Table of Contents. Choose an automatic style from the options provided.

5.13.2 Updating the Table of Contents on Windows

To update your table of contents after making changes to your document, follow these steps:

- Right-click on the table of contents.
- Select "Update Field" from the menu that appears.

5.13.3 Fixing Missing Entries in a Table of Contents on Windows

If you notice some entries are missing from your table of contents, it could be because the headings in your document aren't properly formatted as headings.

- To include a heading in your table of contents, first select the text of the heading you want to add.
- Then, go to the Home tab, click on Styles, and select Heading 1.
- Don't forget to update your table of contents after making any changes to your document.

5.13.4 Creating a Table of Contents on MacOS

Word creates an automatic table of contents based on the headings in your document. If you modify the heading text, level, or sequence, the table of contents can be updated accordingly.

- Position your cursor at the location where you wish to place the table of contents, typically at the start of your document.
- Navigate to the References tab, click on Table of Contents, and select an Automatic Table of Contents style from the available options.

Keep in mind that if you opt for a manual table of contents format, Microsoft Word won't automatically generate your table of contents based on your headings. It will instead use placeholder text for the table, requiring you to manually input every entry.

You have the option to format and customize your table of contents as you see fit. This includes changing the style of the font, adjusting the total number of heading levels displayed, and deciding whether to include dotted lines between page numbers and entries.

5.13.5 Fixing Missing Entries in a Table of Contents on MacOS

Sometimes, when there are missing entries in your table of contents, it's because the headings in your document aren't formatted correctly as headings.

Here's a simple guide to ensure your table of contents reflects the headings in your document correctly:

- Select the text of every heading that you would like to include in the table of contents.
- Navigate to the Home tab, find the Styles section, and select the Heading 1 style for each selected heading.
- After updating the styles, remember to update your table of contents to reflect these changes accurately.

5.14 Working with Captions in Figures, Equations, or Objects

You can label and number various elements in your document by adding captions. A caption typically consists of a label like "Equation," "Table," or "Figure," followed by a letter or number ("a, b, c..." or "1, 2, 3..." generally), and optionally, additional descriptive text. This helps organize and identify figures, equations, tables, and other objects in your document.

5.14.1 Adding Captions

- Click on the item (like a figure, equation, table, etc.) to which you'd like to attach a label.
- Navigate to the References tab and find the Captions section, then select Insert Caption.
- From the drop-down menu, choose the appropriate label that fits the object, like "Equation" or "Figure." If the label you need isn't listed, you can create a new one by selecting "New Label," typing it in, and then clicking OK.
- Enter any text or punctuation that you would like to show after the label.
- Press OK to confirm your changes.

Please note that in Microsoft Word, the caption number is automatically added as a field. If your caption appears as "Figure {SEQ Table * ARABIC}", it means Microsoft

Word is showing field codes instead of field results. To view the caption correctly, press ALT+F9.

5.14.2 Automatic Addition of Captions

Word can automatically add captions to images, tables, or other objects as you insert them into your document.

- First, pick the item you wish to caption, like a figure, equation, or table.
- Then, head to the References tab and click on Insert Caption in the Captions group.
- Simply click on AutoCaption in the Captions dialog box. From there, you can check the boxes for the items you would like Microsoft Word to caption automatically. You also have the option to select where these captions should appear using the Position drop-down list.

5.14.3 Caption a Floating Object

You should group an object and its respective caption if you would like to wrap text around both the object and its caption, or to move them together.

- Place your figure where you want it.

- Opt for Layout Options and pick a text wrapping style.

Remember: complete this step before adding the caption. If you have already added your caption, delete it first, carry out the step above, and then add your caption again.

- Follow the steps outlined earlier to add your caption.
- Click on the caption, press and hold the shift key, and click on the figure to select both.
- To group the items, simply right-click on any of them and select Group, then click on Group from the menu.

Your text should now wrap around the caption and figure smoothly, ensuring they remain together even if their position is changed within the page or document.

Remember that if you reposition a figure, it's a good idea to update the caption numbering to ensure they remain in the right order.

5.14.4 Updating Caption Numbers

When you add a new caption, Microsoft Word will update the caption numbers for you. However, if you move or delete a caption, you'll need to manually initiate a caption update.

- Begin by clicking anywhere within your document, then press CTRL+A to select everything in it.
- Next, right-click and select "Update Field" from the menu that appears. This action will update all the captions throughout your document.

Another way you can update your captions is by selecting the whole document and then pressing the "F9" key.

5.14.5 Formatting Your Captions

After inserting a caption in your Word document, a new style named "Caption" will appear in the style gallery.

- To adjust the formatting of all your captions, proceed to the gallery, right-click on this style, and select "Modify."
- From there, you can customize settings like type, color, and font size for your captions.

5.14.6 Deleting a Caption

To remove a caption, simply select it and hit the delete key. After deleting captions, remember to update any other remaining captions in your Word document.

- To do this, press CTRL+A to select every text, then press the "F9" key. This process will make sure that the caption numbers are accurate after deleting any captions.

5.15 Automatic Table of Figures

You can arrange and list figures, tables, or images in your Microsoft Word document, similar to how you create a table of contents. Start by adding captions to the figures. Then, go to the References tab and select the Insert Table of Figures option. Microsoft Word will scan your document for possible captions and generate a list of figures sorted by page numbers automatically.

Note: Before making a table of figures, ensure you've added captions to every figure and table you want to include in it.

5.15.1 Adding a Table of Figures

- Go to the location in your Word document where you would like the table of figures to appear, and click on that location.
- Navigate to the References tab, and then click on Insert Table of Figures.

If your Word document isn't maximized, you might not see the Insert Table of Figures option. In some minimized views, only the Insert Table of Figures icon is visible.

- Customize the format and options for your table of figures in the Table of Figures dialog box, then click OK.

5.15.2 Updating an Existing Table of Figures

After making any changes, such as adding, moving, altering, or deleting captions, remember to use the Update Table feature to ensure that your table of figures accurately reflects these changes.

- Start by clicking on the table of figures in your Word document to select the whole table.
- Then, navigate to the References tab and click on Update Table.

After clicking on the table of figures in your Word document, you'll see the Update Table option become available. Alternatively, you can press the "F9" key on your keyboard to update the table of figures.

- In the Update Table of Figures dialog box, choose an option to update:

  a) Select "Update page numbers" if you would like to make changes to the page numbers.

b) Select "Update entire table" if you have changed captions or moved figures.

- Click OK to apply your selection.

5.16 Inserting a Cover Page

Word provides a selection of ready-to-use cover pages that can enhance your resume. Simply select a cover page and replace the placeholder text with your own content.

5.16.1 Adding a Cover Page to Your Document on Windows

- Go to the Insert tab and click on Cover Page in the Pages group.
- Choose a cover page layout from the available options in the gallery.
- Once you've added a cover page, you should replace the placeholder text with your own content. Simply click on the section of your cover page you want to edit, like the title, and begin to type your text.

Notes:

- Inserting a different cover page will replace the initial one you added.

- If you need to change a cover page from an older Word version, delete the existing one manually before adding a new cover page from the Word gallery.
- If you want to delete an existing cover page that was inserted with Microsoft Word, go to the Insert tab, then proceed to the Pages group, click on Cover Pages, and select Remove Current Cover Page.

5.16.2 Adding a Cover Page to Your Document on MacOS

Keep in mind that cover pages do not show page numbers.

- Go to the Insert tab and select Cover Page.
- Choose a cover page layout from the available options in the gallery.
- Once you've added a cover page, simply click on the area you want to edit, like the title, and type your own text to replace the placeholder text.

Notes:

- Adding another cover page will replace the initial one you added.
- To preview your cover page's appearance, switch to Web Layout or Print Layout under the View menu.

- If you need to change a cover page from an older Microsoft Word version, delete it manually and add a new cover page from the Word gallery.

5.16.3 Removing a Cover Page

- Go to the Insert tab, choose Cover Page, and then select Remove Cover Page.

5.17 References, Citations, and Bibliography

5.17.1 Adding a Source

- Position your mouse cursor after the text you wish to cite.
- Navigate to the References tab, click on Style, and select a citation style.
- Click on Insert Citation.
- Select Add New Source and enter the details about your source.

5.17.2 Citing Your Source

After you've included a source in your list, you can easily cite it again.

- Position the mouse cursor where you want to cite the text.
- Navigate to the References tab, click on Insert Citation, and select the source you want to cite.
- If you need to include additional details such as page numbers (for a book citation, for instance), click on Citation Options and then choose Edit Citation.

5.17.3 Creating a Bibliography

Now that you've cited your sources in your Word document, it's time to create a bibliography.

- Position your cursor where you would like the bibliography to appear.
- Click on References, then Bibliography, and select a format for your bibliography.

Note: To include a new source in your bibliography, click within the bibliography section and choose "Update Citations and Bibliography" after citing the source.

Chapter 6: Working with Borders, Tables, Rows, and Columns

6.1 Borders

6.1.1 Adding a Border to a Page on Windows

To create a border on a page:

- Click on Design, then choose Page Borders.
- Pick the options for how you'd like the border to appear.
- To change the space between the page's edge and the border, click on Options, adjust the settings as needed, and then click OK.
- Finally, click OK again to apply the changes.

6.1.2 Adding a Border to a Page on MacOS

If you're trying to add a border to a page that's in the center of your Word document, start by inserting section breaks.

- Click on Design, then choose Page Borders.
- In the Borders and Shading box:

  a) On the left under Setting, pick the border style.

  b) Choose None to remove a border.

  c) Select a line style under Style.

  d) Pick a border color using the arrow under Color.

  e) Adjust the width by selecting an option under Width.

- For a clip-art border, click on the arrow under Art and pick a border graphic from the options available.
- Afterward, click on the arrow next to "Apply to" and select "This section - First page only." This option is useful if you intend to add the border to the initial page of the Word document.
- The preview box shows your chosen border styles. To get rid of a border from a specific side, click on the affected line in the Preview box. If you would like to adjust the position of the border on your page, click on Options and tweak the margin settings.
- Once done, click OK to apply the changes.

6.1.3 Removing a Page Border on Windows

To get rid of a border, switch the page border setting to "None."

- Click on the Design tab and select Page Borders.
- In the dialog box labeled "Borders and Shading," pick the page(s) from the Apply to list where you intend to delete the border.
- In the Settings section, pick None.
- Then, click OK to apply the changes.

6.1.4 Removing a Page Border on MacOS

To remove a border from a page in your Word document, simply set the page border setting to none.

- Navigate to Design, then click Page Borders.
- Next, go to the Page Border tab in the Borders and Shading box.
- Click on the arrow beside "Apply to," then pick the page(s) from which you would like to delete the border.
- In the Settings section, choose None, and then click OK to apply changes.

6.1.5 Adding a Border to Specific Text on Windows

At times, placing a border around text can be more effective in your document than using a one-cell table or a text box, achieving an almost identical appearance.

- Highlight a paragraph, line, or word.
- Click on Home, then Borders, and open the border choices menu.
- Pick the type of border you prefer.

6.1.5.1 Customizing the Chosen Border on Windows

- Once you've chosen your text and the basic border type, revisit the Borders menu and select Borders and Shading.
- Choose your preferred width, color, and style, then apply these selections using the buttons in the dialog box's Preview section. Once the preview looks right to you, click OK to confirm.

Ensure that the Apply to box is set correctly to either paragraph or text.

6.1.6 Adding a Border to Specific Text on MacOS

You have the option to add a border to a whole paragraph, a text line, or even just one word. You can make the borders simple or elaborate according to your preference. Additionally, you can apply borders to individual pages, tables, or pictures as needed.

- Select a specific paragraph, line, or word.
- Click on the arrow beside the Borders button located on the Home tab.
- Select the border style you wish to use from the Borders gallery.

6.1.6.1 Customizing the Text Border on MacOS

- Once you've chosen the text and decided on the basic border style you prefer, click on the arrow beside the Borders button, and then select Borders and Shading.
- Proceed to the Borders and Shading dialog box to adjust the width, color, style, and setting options to create the border style you prefer.

Make sure the border style is applied correctly by setting it to either paragraph or text in the "Apply to" section. If no text is selected, the setting will default to paragraph.

- Finally, click on the OK button to apply the changes.

Here's a trick: You can add color to your text's background. Go to the Borders and Shading dialog box, and click on Shading. Choose a color and a pattern from the Fill and Style lists, respectively. The color you pick will fill the selected area with that color, and the pattern you choose will be applied to the area.

6.2 Tables

6.2.1 Inserting a Table

- To create a simple table, go to the Insert menu and click on Table. Then, hover your cursor over the grid until you've selected the desired number of rows and columns.
- To create a bigger or personalized table, click on Insert, then Table, and finally Insert Table.

Here are a couple of tips:

- If you've got text that's already separated by tabs, you can easily turn it into a table. Just go to Insert, then Table, and choose Convert Text to Table.
- If you want to draw your own table from scratch, go to Insert, then Table, and select Draw Table.

6.2.2 Change Text into a Table or Turn a Table into Text

To change text into a table or vice versa, begin by clicking on the Show or Hide paragraph mark button located on the Home tab. This will reveal how the text is divided within your Word document.

6.2.3 Changing Text into a Table

Add separator characters like tabs or commas to show where the text should be split into table columns. Remember, if your text already has commas, you should make use of tabs as separators.

Use paragraph marks to signify where you would like each new table row to start.

- Pick the text you wish to convert, then go to Insert, click on Table, and choose Convert Text to Table.
- Select your preferences in the Convert Text to Table options.
- In the table size settings, ensure that the numbers correspond to the desired rows and columns.
- In the AutoFit behavior settings, select the appearance you prefer for your table. Microsoft Word will automatically set the column widths, but you can adjust them by choosing from these options:

a) To set the same width for every column, enter or choose a value in the Fixed column width box.

b) Click on "AutoFit to Contents" to adjust the column widths based on the text inside each column.

c) To automatically adjust the table size when the available space width changes, such as in landscape orientation or web layout, use AutoFit to Window.

- In the Separate Text At option, select the separator character that matches what was used in your text.
- Next, click on OK. Your text will now be converted to a table.

6.2.4 Changing Table to Text

- Choose the table or rows you wish to turn into text.
- Go to the Layout tab and click on Convert to Text in the Data section.
- Under "Separate text with" within the Convert to Text dialog box, select the separator character you prefer to replace the column boundaries. Each row will be split up by paragraph marks.
- Then, click OK.

6.2.5 Apply Table Styles to Format the Whole Table

Once you've created a table, you can format it entirely using table styles. Hover over each preformatted style to preview how your table will appear.

- Select the table you wish to format.
- Go to the Design tab under Table Tools.
- Hover over every table style in the Table Styles group until you locate one that suits your preference. Click the More arrow to view additional styles.

- Click on the desired style to apply it to your table.
- Then, choose or deselect the checkbox beside every table element in the Table Style Options group to add or remove the selected style.

6.2.6 Adding a Cell to Your Table

- Click on a cell that's positioned directly above or to the right of where you would like to add a new cell.
- Navigate to the Rows & Columns Dialog Box Launcher on the Layout tab under Table Tools and click on it.
- Choose any of the options below:

a) Select "Shift cells to the right" to add a cell and shift all remaining cells in that row to the right. Be aware that using this feature could lead to a row having more cells compared to other rows.

b) Select "Shift cells down" to add a cell and shift every other cell in that column downward by one row each. This action will create a new row at the bottom of the table to accommodate the last cell in that column.

c) To add a new row directly above the cell you clicked on, select "Insert entire row."

d) Select the option labeled "Insert entire column" to add a new column directly beside the cell where you clicked.

6.2.7 Adding a Column to Your Table

- First, select a cell positioned either to the left or right of where you wish to insert a column.
- Then, navigate to the Layout tab under Table Tools.
- Here are two options to add a column, depending on your preference:

  a) To insert a column to the left of the clicked cell, go to the Rows and Columns group and choose "Insert Left."

  b) To insert a column to the right of the clicked cell, navigate to the Rows and Columns group and select "Insert Right."

6.2.8 Adding a Row to Your Table

- First, click on a cell positioned either above or below where you intend to insert a new row.
- Next, navigate to the Layout tab under Table Tools.
- Here are two options to add a row, depending on where you clicked:

  a) To insert a row above the clicked cell, go to the Rows and Columns group and select "Insert Above."

b) To insert a row below the clicked cell, go to the Rows and Columns group and choose "Insert Below."

6.2.9 Deleting a Column, Row, or Cell from Your Table

- Here's what you can do:

  a) To choose a cell, simply click on its left edge.

  b) To choose a column, click on its top border or top gridline.

  c) To pick a row, just click to the row's left.

- Navigate to the Layout tab under Table Tools.
- Click on Delete within the Rows & Columns group, then choose either Delete Cells, Delete Columns, or Delete Rows, depending on your needs.

6.2.10 Merging Cells

Merge multiple cells in a column or row to create a single cell. For instance, combine cells horizontally to make a table header that covers multiple columns.

- To combine cells in a table, start by clicking on the left edge of the first cell. Then, drag your cursor across the other cells you wish to merge.

- Next, go to the Layout tab under Table Tools, and find the Merge Cells option in the Merge group. Click on it to merge the selected cells together.

6.2.11 Splitting Cells

- To divide cells in a table, begin by clicking on a cell or selecting several cells you wish to split.
- Then, navigate to the Layout tab under Table Tools and locate the Split Cells option in the Merge group. Click it to split the selected cells as desired.
- Specify how many rows or columns you want to divide the selected cells into.

6.2.12 Inserting Column Breaks

When you format a Word document that has columns, like in certain newsletter designs, your text will naturally flow from one column to the next. To have more control over your document's layout, you can manually insert column breaks where needed.

- To insert a column break, position your cursor where you want the break to occur.
- Then, click on the "Layout" tab and select "Breaks." For Word 2013 users, click on "Page Layout" and then choose "Breaks."

- After clicking "Breaks," a menu will appear showing different options. Choose "Column" from this menu to insert a column break.
- To view the column break in your document, click on "Home" and then select "Show/Hide."

Here's a handy tip: You can quickly insert a column break by using the keyboard shortcut Ctrl+Shift+Enter at the location of your cursor.

6.3 Lists

In Word, lists can help organize information clearly. For example, you can use numbered or bulleted lists for things like grocery items, making it easier for you and others to read and understand the content.

6.3.1 Creating a Numbered or Bulleted List

- To begin a numbered list, simply type "1." followed by a space, a period, and your text. Word will then automatically initiate the numbered list for you.
- If you type an asterisk (*) followed by a space before your text, Microsoft Word will create a bulleted list for you automatically.
- To finish the list, hit the Enter key on your keyboard until the numbering or bullets are no longer applied.

6.3.2 Using Existing Text to Create a List

Here's how to turn your text into a list:

- Highlight the text you would like to convert into a list.
- Then, go to the "Home" tab and click on either "Numbering" or "Bullets."

Note: You can explore various numbering formats and bullet styles by clicking the downward arrow beside "Numbering" or "Bullets."

6.3.3 Toggle Automatic Numbering or Bullets On/Off

Word automatically detects when you type "1." or an asterisk to begin a numbered or bulleted list. If you prefer, you can disable this automatic list recognition feature.

- Click on "File" and then choose "Options."
- Select "Proofing" and then click on "AutoCorrect Options." Navigate to the "AutoFormat As You Type" tab.
- Choose whether you want to enable or disable automatic numbered or bulleted lists.
- After making your selection, click "OK" to apply the changes.

6.4 Endnotes and Footnotes

Footnotes typically reside at the page's bottom, while endnotes are found at a document's conclusion. They correspond with reference marks in the text, typically in the form of numbers or symbols.

6.4.1 Creating Endnotes and Footnotes in Your Document

- To add a footnote or endnote to your document, first click or tap where you want to place it.
- Then, go to the References tab and choose Insert Footnote for footnotes or Insert Endnote for endnotes.
- Once you've added a footnote or endnote, you'll see it at the bottom of the page or at the end of your document.
- Simply type in the information you desire to include in the footnote or endnote.
- To go back to editing your document, double-click on the reference mark that appears at the start of the footnote or endnote.

6.5 Shapes

In Word, you have the option to include shapes like arrows, circles, and boxes in your documents.

6.5.1 Adding Shapes to Your Document

- Click on the Insert tab, then choose the Shapes icon.
- Pick a shape from the options shown, then click and drag in your workspace to draw that shape.

Note: If you want to make a circle or square without changing its proportions, hold down the Shift key while dragging.

6.6 Pictures

As you become more familiar with Microsoft Word, you might want to include images in your documents. This can be done by either finding one online or by choosing from your own collection. Here are the steps to do so:

6.6.1 Inserting Pictures on Windows

- Choose one of these options:

  a) Go to "Insert," then "Pictures," and select "This Device" to add a picture from your computer.

  b) Navigate to "Insert," then "Pictures," and "Stock Images" for professional-quality backgrounds or images.

  c) Click on "Insert," then "Pictures," and "Online Pictures" to add a picture from the internet.

- Choose the image you prefer, then click on "Insert."

6.6.2 Inserting Pictures on MacOS

- First, click on the spot in the document where you would like the picture to appear.
- Then, go to the Insert tab and select Pictures.
- Choose the method you prefer for adding pictures.

You can use the Photo Browser option to view photo sets saved on your Mac, like those in Photo Booth or iPhoto. Alternatively, the Picture from File option allows you to browse your Mac's files to find photos.

- Once you've located the picture you like, simply drag it from the Photo Browser and drop it into your Word document. Alternatively, you can click on "Insert" in the file browser to add the image.

Remember, the image is added directly to your Word document. If the image is too big and increases your document's size excessively, you can shrink the document by linking to the image instead of adding it directly. Just check the "Link to File" option in the Choose a Picture dialog box.

6.6.3 Wrapping Text Around a Picture on Windows

- First, click on the picture you want to work with.
- Then, choose "Layout Options" from the menu.
- From there, pick the layout style that suits your needs best.

When you choose "In Line with Text" for your picture, it behaves like regular text within a paragraph. This means it shifts position along with your text. Alternatively, selecting other options allows you to move the picture freely on the page while text wraps around it.

This simple process allows you to customize how your picture interacts with the surrounding text in your document.

6.6.4 Wrapping Text Around a Picture or Object on MacOS

- First, choose the object or picture you want to adjust.
- Then, navigate to either Shape Format or Picture Format, depending on what you're working with.
- From there, click on Arrange and then Wrap Text to modify how text interacts with the object or picture.

Select the wrapping options that suit your needs. Options include Behind Text, Top and Bottom, and In Line with Text. These choices determine how your picture interacts with the surrounding text in your document.

6.6.5 Resizing a Picture

- To adjust the size of an image, click on the image and then drag one of the corner handles.

6.6.6 Cropping the Edges of a Picture on Windows

- Click on Insert and then Picture to place the desired picture in your document.
- After inserting the picture, right-click on it. A menu will pop up with options; look for the crop button among them.
- Click on the crop button. This action will display black crop handles along the corners and edges of the selected picture.
- To crop the picture, you can carry out one of the following actions:

  a) To crop one side, pull the side cropping handle inward.

  b) To crop equally on two sides that run parallel, hold down the Ctrl key and then drag inward on the side cropping handle.

  c) To crop two sides together, just pull inwards on the corner cropping tool.

Note: You can expand the area around a picture by dragging the cropping handles outward, a technique known as outcropping.

- If you want to adjust the crop area, you can do so by dragging the corners or edges of the crop rectangle or by moving the picture itself.
- Once you're done, click anywhere outside the cropped picture in your document or press the Esc key on your keyboard.

Note: While shapes can't be cropped directly, you can still achieve a similar effect by resizing the shape and using the Edit Points tool. This allows you to customize the shape or create a cropping-like effect.

6.6.7 Cropping the Edges of a Picture on MacOS

- To add an image to a Word document, go to the Insert tab and select Pictures.
- Once the image is inserted, click on it, then navigate to the toolbar ribbon and click on the Picture Format tab.
- Once you're on the Picture Format tab, choose Crop. This action will display black crop handles around the corners and edges of the selected picture, allowing you to adjust the cropping as needed.

- To crop the picture, simply drag any of the crop handles inward. If you use a corner handle, it will crop two adjacent sides simultaneously.
- After making your adjustments, click outside the image to view the cropped picture.

Keep in mind that when you crop an image, the parts you cut out are hidden but still saved within the file.

Chapter 7: Document Management

7.1 Saving Your Word Document

Make sure to save your document to avoid losing your progress, then print it out if you intend sharing it with others.

- To save your document, go to the File menu, then click Save.

- Choose a folder where you want to save it, enter a name in the file's name space, and then click Save again.

- Remember to save your work frequently by pressing Ctrl+S.

- To print your document, first click on the File tab, then select Print.

7.2 Printing Your Word Document

Before printing, you have the option of previewing your document and choosing specific pages for printing.

7.2.1 Previewing the Document

- Click on File, then choose Print.

- Use the arrows at the bottom of the page to navigate forward and backward to preview each page.
Tip: If the text appears too small, adjust the zoom slider to make it larger. You will find the zoom slider at the bottom of the page.

- Select the desired number of copies, adjust any other settings you need, and then click on the Print button.

7.2.2 Printing Individual Pages

To print specific pages, follow these steps:

- Click on File, then choose Print.
- If you want to print specific pages, adjust document properties, or include tracked changes and comments when printing, click the arrow next to "Print All Pages" in the Settings menu. This will show you all the available printing options to choose from.
- When you're printing documents and need to be selective about which pages to print, you have a few options:

a) If you want to print just the page you're looking at in the preview, choose "Print Current Page."

b) For printing a series of pages in order, such as 1 to 3, click on "Custom Print." In the Pages box, type the first and last page numbers.

c) If you need to print single pages and a range of pages together, such as page 5 and pages 7 to 10, click on "Custom Print" and type in your page numbers and ranges with commas, like this: 5, 7-10.

7.3 Sharing Your Word Document

If you use Microsoft Office with Outlook as your default email, you can easily send a Word document as an attachment in your email. Additionally, from Microsoft Word, you can directly send your file as the email's main content. Just ensure that Outlook is set as your default email app for this feature to work smoothly.

7.3.1 Sending Your Document as an Attachment

- Navigate to the 'File' menu and select 'Share.' From there, you'll find different options available based on the specific Office application you are using.
- Option one lets you upload your file to OneDrive, giving you the flexibility to share it via a direct link or email. Option two allows you to attach the file as a PDF or directly to an email.
- Simply enter the recipients' email addresses, adjust the subject line and message content as needed, and then hit the "Send" button.

7.4 Secure your Document by Adding a Password

To secure a document, you can set a password for it. Passwords are sensitive to uppercase and lowercase letters and can be up to 15 characters in length. It's advisable to create a robust password that you can easily recall. However, for added safety, keep a backup of it in a secure location.

If you happen to forget or misplace your document's password, Word doesn't offer a way to retrieve it. If your IT administrators have used the DocRecrypt tool before setting the document password, they may be able to assist with password retrieval.

7.4.1 Adding a Password on Windows

- Open your document and navigate to File, then click on Info.
- Choose Protect Document and select Encrypt with Password.
- Enter your chosen password, click OK, confirm the password, and then click OK again to finalize it.
- Be sure to save your file after setting the password to ensure that the password is applied.

7.4.2 Adding a Password on MacOS

- Navigate to the Review tab and click on Protect Document to access the protection options for your document.

- Once you're on the Review tab, look for the option "Protect Document," which will be highlighted.

- Proceed to Security. From there, you can choose to set passwords for opening the document, making modifications, or both.

- Confirm each password by entering it again, then click OK to apply the settings.

7.5 Closing Your Microsoft Word Document

Closing a Microsoft Word document is quite simple. Here's a straightforward guide to help you do it:

- Ensure that all your work is saved by clicking on the "Save" button or pressing Ctrl + S.
- Once your document is saved, you can close it by clicking on the "X" button in the top right corner of the window. Alternatively, you can use the keyboard shortcut Alt + F4.
- If you have multiple documents open and want to close only one, click on the document's tab and then follow the steps mentioned above.

7.6 Restoring a Previous Version of a Word File

When AutoRecover is enabled, your file gets saved automatically as you work on it, creating versions that can be recovered based on when they were saved.

7.6.1 Recovering a Saved File

- Begin by opening the document you were last working on.
- Next, click on the "File" tab, followed by selecting "Info."

- Look for the section titled "Manage Documents" and choose the file labeled "when I closed without saving."
- At the top bar of the file, choose "Restore" to replace any existing saved versions with the selected one. Alternatively, you can opt to compare versions by selecting "Compare" instead of "Restore."

7.6.2 Recovering a File That Wasn't Saved

To recover an unsaved document in Microsoft Word, follow these steps:

- Navigate to File, then click on Info, followed by Manage Document, and then choose Recover Unsaved Documents.
- Select the file you want to recover, and then click Open.
- Once the document is open, click on Save As in the top bar to save the file to your desired location.

Chapter 8: Making Your Work Easier

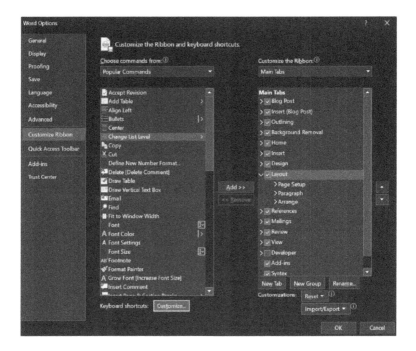

Here are a few quick tips for speeding up your typing in Microsoft Word. These shortcuts may vary in their effectiveness depending on whether you're using the online version, mobile app, or Microsoft 365.

8.1 General Keyboard Shortcuts for Windows

1. Press **Ctrl + A** to select everything.

2. Use **Ctrl + B** to make text bold.

3. Copy text with **Ctrl + C**.

4. **Ctrl + D** changes character formatting.

5. Align text in the center by pressing **Ctrl + E**.

6. **Ctrl + F** helps you find specific words.

7. Go to a particular location with **Ctrl + G**.

8. **Ctrl + H** is for replacing text.

9. Make text italicized using **Ctrl + I**.

10. Justify text alignment with **Ctrl + J**.

11. Use **Ctrl + K** to add a hyperlink.

12. Left-align text by pressing **Ctrl + L**.

13. Indent text with **Ctrl + M**.

14. **Ctrl + N** creates a new document.

15. Open a document using **Ctrl + O**.

16. Print your document with **Ctrl + P**.

17. Remove paragraph formatting using **Ctrl + Q**.

18. Right-justify text with **Ctrl + R**.

19. Save your work by pressing **Ctrl + S**.

20. Create a hanging indent (tab) with **Ctrl + T**.

21. Press **Ctrl + U** to underline text.

22. Paste content using **Ctrl + V**.

23. Close the document with **Ctrl + W**.

24. Cut text with **Ctrl + X**.

25. Redo a previously undone action using **Ctrl + Y**.

26. Undo an action with **Ctrl + Z**.

27. Single-space lines by pressing **Ctrl + 1**.

28. Double-space lines using **Ctrl + 2**.

29. Set 1.5-line spacing with **Ctrl + 5**.

30. Decrease font size by 1 point using **Ctrl + Left Bracket [**

31. Increase font size by 1 point with **Ctrl + Right Bracket]**.

32. Convert selected text to all capital letters using **Ctrl + Shift + A**.

33. Apply double underline to selected text with **Ctrl + Shift + D**.

34. Enable or disable revision tracking using **Ctrl + Shift + E**.

35. Open the font window with **Ctrl + Shift + F**.

36. Create a bullet point using **Ctrl + Shift + L**.

37. View or hide non-printing characters with **Ctrl + Shift + ***.

38. Increase font size with **Ctrl + Shift + >**.

39. Decrease font size with **Ctrl + Shift + <**.

40. Increase font size using **Ctrl +]**.

41. Decrease font size using **Ctrl + [**.

42. Insert a cent sign (¢) with **Ctrl + / + C**.

43. Delete the word to the right of the cursor using **Ctrl + Del**.

44. Delete the word to the left of the cursor with **Ctrl + Backspace**.

45. Move the cursor to the end of your document using **Ctrl + End**.

46. Move the cursor to the beginning of your document with **Ctrl + Home**.

47. Reset highlighted text to the default font using **Ctrl + Spacebar**.

48. Insert a page break with **Ctrl + Enter**.

49. Save the document under a new name with **Alt + F, A**.

50. Show the Unicode code of a highlighted character using **Alt + X**.

51. Press **Shift + Enter** to add a soft break, not a new paragraph.

52. Use **Shift + Insert** to paste.

53. Press **Shift + Alt + D** to insert today's date.

54. For the current time, use **Shift + Alt + T**.

55. Cancel a command by pressing **Esc**.

8.2 General Keyboard Shortcuts on MacOS

1. Press **Command + N** to make a new file or item, depending on the context.

2. Use **Shift + Command + P** to create a new file from a template or theme.

3. **Command + Option + R** expands or minimizes the ribbon.

4. Press **Command + S** to save or sync your work.

5. To print, use **Command + P**.

6. **Command + O** opens an item or file.

7. **Command + W** closes the current item or file.

8. **Command + Q** quits the current application.

9. Press **Command + H** to hide the current application.

10. Use **Option + Command + H** to hide other applications.

11. **Command + M** minimizes the window you're working in.

8.3 MacOS Shortcuts to Format and Edit Contents

1. Use **Command + Z** to undo the last change you made.

2. Press **Command + Y** to redo or repeat the last action.

3. **Command + X** cuts the selection and copies it to the clipboard.

4. **Command + C** copies the selected content to the clipboard.

5. To copy the formatting from the selection, use **Command + Shift + C**.

6. **Control + Option + C** copies the selection to the Scrapbook.

7. **Command + V** pastes the copied content.

8. For a special paste (not available in all products), use **Command + Control + V**.

9. **Command + Shift + V** pastes formatting to the selection.

10. **Command + A** selects all content.

11. Press **Command + F** to find specific content.

12. Use **Command + K** to insert a hyperlink.

8.4 Function Key-Specific Keyboard Shortcuts

These shortcuts are applicable if your keyboard includes function keys.

1. Press **F1** to access the help panel.

2. Use **Shift + F1** to open the reveal formatting panel.

3. Press **Alt + F1** to move to the next field.

4. Use **Alt + Shift + F1** to move to the previous field.

5. Press **F2** to relocate text or objects.

6. Use **Ctrl + F2** to open the print window.

7. Press **Alt + Shift + F2** to save your document.

8. Use **Alt + Ctrl + F2** to bring up the open window.

9. Press **F3** to expand an AutoText entry.

10. Use **Alt + F3** to create an AutoText entry.

11. Pressing **Shift + F3** changes the case of the text you've selected.

12. Using **Ctrl + F3** cuts the selected text and moves it to the Spike.

13. Pressing **Ctrl + Shift + F3** inserts the contents of the Spike.

14. To repeat your last action, simply press **F4**.

15. **Shift + F4** will repeat the last "Find" action you performed.

16. **Ctrl + F4** closes the current document you're working on.

17. If you want to quit Microsoft Word entirely, press **Alt + F4**.

18. Pressing **F5** opens the "Go To" tab on the Find and Replace window.

19. To move to the previous edit made in the document, use **Shift + F5**.

20. **Ctrl + Shift + F5** opens the Bookmark window for easy navigation.

21. Use **F6** to navigate to the next frame or pane in your Word window.

22. Press **Shift + F6** to go back to the previous frame or pane.

23. **Ctrl + F6** will take you to the next open document window.

24. To switch to the previous open document window, press **Ctrl + Shift + F6**.

25. **F7** will open the Editor pane for a grammar and spelling check.

26. **Shift + F7** opens the thesaurus for word suggestions.

27. **Alt + F7** helps you find the next spelling or grammar error.

28. **Alt + Shift + F7** opens the Translation pane for language assistance.

29. **F8** puts Word in selection mode to expand a selection.

30. Use **Shift + F8** to reduce a selection's size.

31. To select a column, use **Ctrl + Shift + F8**.

32. Press **F9** to update a field in your document.

33. **Shift + F9** reveals the code behind a field.

34. **Ctrl + F9** inserts new Empty Field {} braces.

35. Use **Ctrl + Shift + F9** to unlink a field from its source.

36. **Alt + F9** toggles the display of a field's underlying code.

37. Press **F10** to show key tips for navigation.

38. **Shift + F10** displays a context menu for the selected item.

39. **Ctrl + F10** maximizes the document window for easier viewing.

40. **Alt + Shift + F10** brings up a window or menu related to your current selection.

41. Use **F11** to move to the next field in your document.

42. **Shift + F11** takes you to the previous field in your document.

43. **Ctrl + F11** locks a field to prevent editing.

44. **Ctrl + Shift + F11** unlocks a previously locked field.

45. **Alt + Shift + F11** opens the Microsoft Script Editor.

46. **F12** opens the Save As window for saving your document with a new name.

47. **Shift + F12** quickly saves your document.

48. **Ctrl + F12** opens the Open window to access other documents.

49. **Ctrl + Shift + F12** opens the Print window to manage printing settings.

Conclusion

Let's wrap up your Microsoft Word journey with a concise conclusion that ties together the key points for beginners and experts alike.

Microsoft Word serves as a foundational tool for anyone venturing into the world of word processing. It offers a user-friendly interface with a multitude of features to enhance document creation. As beginners navigate through the basics, mastering functions like text formatting, page layout adjustments, and document saving becomes pivotal.

Furthermore, understanding keyboard shortcuts such as Command + N for creating new files or Command + Z for undoing actions can significantly streamline workflows. Familiarizing oneself with these shortcuts empowers users to work efficiently and save time.

As beginners progress, exploring advanced features like templates, styles, and collaboration tools expands their Word proficiency. Templates provide pre-designed layouts for various document types, whereas styles ensure consistency in formatting across documents. Collaborative features enable real-time editing and commenting, enhancing teamwork and productivity.

Moreover, learning how to insert images, tables, etc. adds versatility to document design. Utilizing these elements effectively improves the visual appeal and readability of documents.

Lastly, continuous practice and exploration are key to mastering Microsoft Word. Engaging with online tutorials, experimenting with different functionalities, and seeking assistance from the Help menu or online communities further enriches one's Word skills.

In essence, Microsoft Word empowers beginners with essential tools and functionalities to create, edit, and present documents professionally. With dedication and practice, mastering Word becomes an attainable goal, unlocking a world of possibilities in document creation and management.

END

Thank you for reading my book.

Aaron J. Reiss

www.ingramcontent.com/pod-product-compliance
Lightning Source LLC
LaVergne TN
LVHW051243050326
832903LV00028B/2549